A Manifesto of Peace
Light on the Path of an Emissary of Peace

A Manifesto of Peace
Light on the Path of an Emissary of Peace

by

Rev. Michael Beckwith, D.D.

"Blessed are the peacemakers, for they will be called children of God."

Holy Bible

Compiled and edited by
Anita Rehker

Agape Publishing, Inc.
Culver City, California

Copyright 2002 by Michael Beckwith

Published, printed and distributed in the
United States of America
by

Agape Publishing, Inc.
5700 Buckingham Parkway
Culver City, California 90230
(310) 348-1250 www.agapeonline.org

All rights reserved. No part of this book may be used or reproduced in any from without prior written permission of the publisher except in the case of brief quotations embodied in articles and reviews.

Publisher's Note

Dear Reader,

During this challenging time in the history of our human family, it is with great love that Agape Publishing offers to hungry hearts a compilation of wisdom and comfort from Rev. Dr. Michael's services, interviews, personal conversations, correspondence, contemplation, meditations and prayer. May what follows be of the highest service to you in your walk as a peacemaker, in your divine call as an emissary of peace living in a worldspace that truly is without boundaries.

A Manifesto of Peace
Light on the Path of an Emissary of Peace

*O*n this round planet there are no sides; we are planetary citizens inhabiting the earth under the sovereignty of the Eternal and its universal laws. Boundaries that separate people from people, country from country are artificial demarcations drawn in the sands of time by the forceful human hand—never did the Divine Architect design such divisions. There is not an individual on the planet who has not been affected by the September 11th terrorist attacks in America. Every soul is on a perpetual pilgrimage to an ever-expanding realization of oneness with the All. What results is a vulnerable heart open so widely in compassion that one cries out for all humanity as one's very own, one loves and serves all humanity as one's very own.

Each of us is on the planet at this stage in its evolution because of what is endeavoring to be birthed in, as and through us. We are individualized expressions of "God with skin" who have taken incarnation to provide evidence of the Living Presence of unconditional love, intelligence, compassion, peace. Time comes to us in the form of experiences that birth in our consciousness—individually and collectively—a new dimension of how to live on the earth. Our earthly assignment is to hold a consciousness of openness and receptivity so that Infinite Mind may download Itself through humanity. We have progressed enough spiritually and scientifically to understand the paradox that although we may have to serve the goal of peace for a long time, it can instantaneously occur if the field of collective consciousness is fertile enough!

The path of an emissary of peace is an all-inclusive one where there exists a sufficiency of love and compassion for both the victims of violence and its perpetrators. In the mind of an emissary of peace there is an understanding that perpetrators of violence are also its victims—victims of their own inner hatred. Human nature is inclined to resist such an approach in fear that this may free wrongdoers from accountability. Be assured that the simultaneity of compassion for victim and perpetrator alike does not prevent the wheels of Divine Justice from turning. What it does do is affect change in the consciousness of all—one's own, victims and perpetrators.

I say this not to be controversial—I know well enough the contrariness of this statement to the dictates of human opinion! But we must remind ourselves that we are not only human beings; we are made in the image and likeness of God, spiritual beings having a human incarnation. I am not encouraging us to in any way deny the horror of what occurred on September 11th—not at all! Who among us does not weep for those who have lost their loved ones in such a tragically violent way? It would be heartless not to deeply feel their suffering.

Pray, and pray often for those who were literally catapulted out of the body temple. Their consciousness will be comforted by your loving vibrations of Godspeed, love and friendship. Pray also for their loved ones, affirming that their spirits have the faith, strength and courage to carry on. It is not difficult to place ourselves in their hearts and feel their anguish.

Honoring the Stages of Grief

We cannot deny the emotional upheaval that is going on within our nation at this time. We are in the midst of a grieving process, a deep collective sorrow over these tragic events that have claimed the lives of so many. Loss on such a massive scale causes fear, a fear that we are no longer safe in our world, that the world is out of control and certainly beyond our individual sphere of influence.

Anger is also a natural reaction to grief. Examining the texture of this anger through prayer and meditation can so expand the heart that anger becomes transmuted into what the Buddhists call *bodhichitta*, an opened heart. From the ashes of what appears to be destruction on the American landscape, a shift in consciousness may occur that will herald a global society of lovers, of selfless givers, of emissaries of peace. Then we may say with Pythagoras, "Take courage, the human race is divine."

Although not everyone experiences the stages of grief in quite the same order, it is common for anger to give way to guilt. I heard some individuals on television expressing their guilt over remaining unharmed while so many lost their lives or were injured. Others experienced guilt because a change in their personal plans required a loved one to be in or near the World Trade Center or on an airplane and thereby a victim of tragedy.

We are often called to respect the awesome mystery of life. There is a place where the mind stops, where our spiritual arrogance halts in the face of That which is the All. The remedy for fear, anger, guilt and confusion is faith, a faith in That which is beyond any spiritual concept that can be thought or verbalized. Relief from the burden of guilt comes from placing our faith in That which created us and ever responds to us. **Rest in the assurance that no experience comes to punish or test us. Experience comes to awaken us.**

Temples, mosques, synagogues and churches are functioning as hospitals of the heart bringing light, love and compassion to our temporary darkness. Whatever your path or practice, consider increasing the amount of time you devote to daily prayer and meditation because this is what will assist you in accessing the spiritual dimension of your being for processing the emotions and feelings you are experiencing. During intense emotional challenges, it is sometimes difficult to sufficiently calm down and turn one's consciousness within. It is at these times that we rely on grace, a Grace that reads our hearts and looks not at the imperfection of our prayer or meditation.

Few escape the tendency to flow with the current of "group think" in the face of national tragedy and outrage. There is an inclination—perhaps even a subtle pressure to identify with the group reaction. It takes self-control to maintain an expanded state of awareness and courage to break free from the contagion of mob response or vigilante aggression. It is steadfastness in our spiritual practices that moves us through the stages of grief while we simultaneously function as vehicles of order, harmony, peace, love, compassion, forgiveness, right action.

Cultivating a Heart as Wide as the World

This is a time for each of us to open our hearts in great honesty with ourselves. Perhaps we are convinced that our abhorrence of violence prevents us from practicing it. A closer look will reveal that not only do we practice violence on a daily basis, we often escalate it in our personal inner and outer environments. One may be a mental terrorist, inwardly sending bombs of judgment, anger, animosity or prejudice towards a particular person, race or culture. Outwardly, it may manifest as spiteful words or actions. However and wherever violence expresses, it pollutes our environment with toxic vibrations of harm.

Stopping the cycle of violence begins with our relationship with ourselves. If we have a nuclear war going on in our own head, we may expect to have a corresponding battleground in the affairs of our personal life. So ask yourself if you escalate self-violence through negative self-talk, desecrating the divine image in which you were created. Introspect on your thoughts, motives and actions. Excavate the contents of your mind so that any mental or emotional habit patterns that undermine a healthy, mature thinking and response to life may be eradicated. Check in to see—without self-condemnation—where an attitude needs adjusting in order to live more compassionately, to make room in the heart for oneself and others.

I agree with President Bush's poignant statement that "adversity introduces us to ourselves." Adversity gives us a clearer picture of who we are individually and collectively. During and immediately after the tragedy hit, some individuals moved toward a heroic response volunteering their services, gifts and resources—sacrificing even their own lives. Others moved further into hate and crimes of hate such as throwing rocks at mosques, attacking anyone whom they thought reflected the face of the enemy, wore a turban or had a "suspicious" sounding last name. In the process of being introduced to ourselves, we must be courageous enough not to project our own inner shadows onto other individuals or cultures.

Unless we come clean and take responsibility for our individual and collective biases and prejudices, coming together in heroic gestures of generosity, self-sacrifice or patriotic flag waving will not be strong enough to permanently shift us to a new paradigm of world citizenry. Each of us must bravely walk through our own unresolved issues of fear, doubt, worry, insecurity, blame, selfishness, greed, ignorance—all of it! Unless we are willing to do that kind of inner work, the seeming unity we are now witnessing in America will be only temporary.

Tragic occurrences in our country such as the mass murder at Columbine High School, news reports of parents murdering their children, children murdering their parents, children murdering children—reveal the violence flowing in our national bloodstream. Violence in our country did not just begin on September 11th! Nor can the causes of violence be wrapped in a tidy package of blame on the movie industry, drugs imported into America, rap and heavy metal music or rave concerts. It is the mind within the individual that creates the popularity and demand for violent movies, music and drugs. As the sage Krishnamurti pointed out, "The inward strife projected outwardly becomes the world chaos. After all, war is the spectacular result of our everyday life."

The events of September 11th have left us nowhere to hide from the violence in our own society. What are we going to do? How are we going to respond to the Universe's plea to allow peace to find a foothold in our individual hearts so that collectively we may give birth to the possibilities seeking to be born through us? Is our question going to remain at the level of "What is the meaning of a person's death?" Or, will it become "How can I give my life meaning based upon the deaths of so many; what is the purpose of my life?" These questions emerge so that a more profound meaning may come from the heartbreaking loss of so many lives on September 11th.

Asking the right questions activates the universal spiritual law Jesus was referring to when he said, "Ask, and it will be given to you; search, and you will find; knock, and the door will be opened for you. For everyone who asks receives, and everyone who searches finds, and for everyone who knocks the door will be opened." If we want to have a heart as wide as the world, if we want the vibration of global care to express through us, there are penetrating questions that an emissary of peace places before the tribunal of his/her conscience.

There is a method of questioning that directly opens one's consciousness to Divine Guidance. Every scripture confirms that God responds. God's response corresponds to its own nature inherent within us. To receive the broadcast of a bigger answer, we must correspondingly provide a bigger receiving station within our consciousness and give our consent to Divine Guidance.

Here are some questions to gently ask in the mirror of your consciousness:

What feelings did I meet within myself when I first learned of the tragic events?

Am I experiencing a temptation to become snagged into mob-thinking?

Is there a desire to retaliate in a violent way? If so, where is the desire to lash out originating from?

Where am I in the grieving process?

Have forgiveness and compassion seeped into my heart and thoughts?

Do I need to reach out for support, as well as to give it?

Do I expect applause for my contributions, or am I willing to be of service for its own sake?

What kind of world do I want to live in?

What must I release from within my own consciousness to create that kind of world?

What must I do to create that kind of world?

Some individuals may view the questioning process as an assault on the "mom and apple pie" view of our American way of life. Or, perhaps the suggestion to question the actions of our government may appear to be hinting that our capitalistic way of life is to blame for the events of September 11th. On the contrary! One of our most cherished rights is to question. Throughout our history, questioning has preserved our democratic way of life and contributed towards the development of all that is right and good within America's dynamic society of freedom.

So these questions are not meant in any way to indicate that the American way of life drew to itself the terrorist attacks, for that would be casting blame upon the victims as well as all Americans. It is ignorance that is to blame. This devastation is a crisis, and crisis provides an opportunity to wake up on many levels of existence. We might consider it a "9ll" call from the universe to take responsibility for birthing a new way of being on the planet.

Tearing Away the Masks of Pseudo Patriotism

As an emissary of peace, a minister, as Spiritual Director of the Agape International Spiritual Center, I am not about winning a popularity contest. I cannot go lockstep and sell out to a majority point of view to be politically correct or, for that matter, pseudo-patriotic. While I love, appreciate and respect being an American, I know myself to be a world citizen. Socrates put it this way: "I am not Greek, or even Athenian. I am a citizen of the planet earth."

The soul knows no boundaries. Whether one is Irish, Tibetan, South American, Palestinian, American or African—the feelings of sorrow, joy, love—these feel the same to all of us. Even if varied by degree, the essence of these emotions is similarly felt by all beings. **When we hear about our brothers and sisters in other countries being killed in senseless conflicts, it is revealing to notice if we feel the same intensity of pain as we do when Americans are victims.**

Through the pain we now know in America, we can feel the pain of individuals throughout the world who have lost loved ones and citizens to wars, terrorism and other forms of violence. Our pain connects us to the pain of all humanity. Members of our global family in Ireland, Africa, Israel, Sri Lanka, Palestine,[1] Central America, South America—so many live under the threat of war and acts of terrorism as a way of life. America has been free from such oppression within its borders, and, unless one has family or friends living or traveling in these countries, barely a thought is given to what the rest of our global family experiences. We are lulled by the routine of our daily lives. The events of September 11th have forced open our eyes, ears, hearts and collective conscience.

Technology has turned the planet into a neighborhood. Now is the time for its transformation into a sister-and-brotherhood wherein each of us fulfills the responsibility of being a beneficial presence on the planet. An emissary of peace undergoes the necessary discipline of his/her own heart to embrace membership in a worldwide human race, one that does not succumb to the limitation of pseudo-patriotism or prejudice—the byproducts of ignorance. An emissary of peace does not become sucked into a downward spiral of lack of trust in the inherent

Good in the soul of every man, woman and child. Even if one discovers that she/he has been swayed, there is a speedy realignment with the truth that we are cosmic citizens interconnected to all humanity.

We must free ourselves from the influences of ignorance and the prejudices inherent within our respective cultural environments, for what good is patriotism if it destroys life itself? Crucial to this purification process is our prayer and meditation practice which keeps us in a state of choice. Each time we center our consciousness, we have the potential to notice where we have been caught or snagged by worldly opinion, fear, doubt—those emotions that allow us to remain circumscribed by external facts rather than the internal Reality of our own true nature as spiritual beings imbued with the qualities of our Creator.

---

1. Although Palestine is not currently a state, President Bush–and past presidents–have negotiated for a Palestinian homeland.

Renouncing Illusions
of False Power

We are a nation that is encouraged to consume, consume, consume. Even in the face of the economic backlash from September 11th's events we are being told to maintain our level of consumerism as a sign of patriotism. Patriotism has become synonymous with spending. Isn't it time to face and question our relentless pursuit of acquisition and consumption? Not merely from the perspective of materialism, but because many of the items we acquire and consume are destructive to the very ecology upon which human life is dependent.

There is never enough of that which doesn't satisfy. To compulsively or mindlessly consume in an effort to fill up the empty places within ourselves or to compete with the Joneses brings no lasting satisfaction to the inner soul-hunger. Now this doesn't mean that we are not to enjoy lovely things in life. Just as an artist buys canvases and brushes to support his art, so may we materially invest in those items that support our art of living, that enhance our self-care in the physical, mental, emotional and spiritual realms throughout our walk in life. So I invite all of us to examine how we prioritize and allocate our individual monetary resources.

When we sell-out to materialism, spiritual balance is lost and all hell breaks loose on the planet. This is not a statement against prosperity. I say these things to underscore that the foundation of life must be based on spiritual principles from which every good and beautiful thing arises. Many people prepare for their day by finding out what's going on with the stock market rather than anchoring their consciousness in prayer and meditation which produce wisdom-guided action. Spiritual practice is not a Saturday or Sunday affair—to truly evolve there must be a daily disciplining and renewing of the inner spirit.

Something significant was revealed when the perpetrators attacked what they believed symbolized America's gods of power and security. People have been led to believe that the more the Pentagon spends on technologically sophisticated "peace keeping weapons" the more secure we are as a nation. And yet our country was brought to its knees by crude box cutting implements, stripping away in one day the false sense of power and security that comprise the American way of life. How we responded revealed the true soul-power of America: greed and self-centeredness gave way to individuals sacrificing their own lives to save others, to give blood, donate emergency supplies, to pray, to renounce violence. Emissaries of peace act from the consensus that now is the time to replace materialistic values with spiritual values, to replace the economic greed which has raped and pillaged Mother Earth with spiritual principles of love, compassion and reverence for all life.

All around us can be seen the quest to acquire possessions, name, fame—the illusions of false power. Fulfillment at this level occurs so that we may learn that it is simply a pseudo reflection of the genuine security we seek. This is why awakening is called "self-realization," rather than "self attainment." There is nothing for the Self to attain since it contains all that is required for fulfillment. This realization instigates a revolt against the instability of the materialistic values that have been enthroned in humankind's economic, governmental, educational, commercial and even religious structures. As spiritual values preempt materialistic ones, the objects of a spiritually bankrupt society are replaced with those of a spiritually rich one.

Although it is simple it is not easy. As the definitions of the small self to which we are attached melt away, there arises an egoic sense of loss followed by an effort to cling to the identity of name, fame, position, race, gender. But as this false armor is willingly—and sometimes not so willingly dropped, spiritual qualities begin to ooze from the soul and one becomes attuned to the Divine Order of the Universe. Then how easy it is pour out to all beings the universal qualities of peace, love, forgiveness and compassion. The spiritually wise turn worldly values upside down with love!

Spiritualizing Politics

You have heard persons interviewed on television announce that through the recent terrorist attacks "America has lost her innocence." I prefer to say that America has lost her ignorance. Our eyes have been opened to what is a way of life for many of our brothers and sisters on the planet.

On those occasions when I have been blessed to sit with His Holiness the Dalai Lama, he would mention that possibly the American people haven't suffered enough to understand the deeper meaning of compassion. Now he wasn't in any way wishing suffering on Americans. Rather, he was indicating how crisis and its resultant suffering function to provide insights and revelations that create opportunities for change. They come as great awakeners that stir up a questioning process about how we do "business as usual." While our country has historically provided goods and assistance during international emergencies, in our own backyard we have been able to conduct our professional and social lives as usual. Up until this time we have experienced a sense of safety in America that, while being a tremendous blessing, has prevented us from compassionately comprehending what millions in our world experience as a way of life.

After the events of September 11th, how can we ever again ignore the suffering right within America and that of our global brothers and sisters? We can no longer afford not to recognize that each of us is an essential part of the collective consciousness that impacts the entire planet. As we evolve to this state of consciousness we move closer to the enlightened realization of Jesus the Christ when he said, "As I am lifted up, I draw all unto me." He was describing the quantum field that demonstrates how each one of us affects as many as 100,000 people. The question is, are we willing to do the inner spiritual work required to raise our consciousness to a vibrational frequency of unconditional love, forgiveness and compassion that dissolve the sense of separation from the Life that lives within every man, woman and child on the planet?

Our intimate human relationships exist so that we may practice unconditional love and expand it to include the entire planet. To paraphrase Dr. Howard Thurman, it is impossible to love humanity "in general." Humanity must be loved "in particular," which means that we first learn to love the people right next to us regardless of the color of their skin, the shape of their bodies, their sexual orientation, the religion they practice or their political affiliation. Just walking down the street looking into the faces of those with whom we come in contact and witnessing what arises in our minds quickly reveals how close we are to loving "in particular."

When world leaders sever a working partnership with universal principles they flounder without a spiritual compass to guide their course in the best interest of humanity. The sacred is to govern the secular. Mohandas K. Gandhi, Dr. Martin Luther King and Nelson Mandela revolutionized their societies by their spiritualized understanding of life. They taught us that there is no separation between our political endeavors, social endeavors and spiritual endeavors—all are to be governed by the principle of Truth that we are indeed one global family co-creating the destiny of our planet.

Recently I was reading *The Three Faces of Power*, a spiritually intelligent book written by a Quaker, Ken Boulding. Mr. Boulding describes the highest form of power as being "integrative power". This translates into making conscious choices to think and act from Universal Principle. It is the opposite of the lesser forms of power which are based on a sense of separation that threaten: "Do this or else we will bomb and force economic sanctions upon you," or 50/50 bargaining—"you do this for us and we'll do that for you," the results of which are at best temporary.

Integrative power results from choosing Divine Right Action which opens a space for dialogue leading to union rather than separation. No one is excluded from the communication about sharing the world's resources. Is it not obvious that the global family is at a stage where decision-making must be inclusive of the overall good of the whole?

If today's leaders of the world's governments sat among self-realized beings such as Buddha, Jesus, Krishna and Mohammed, they would be strongly exhorted not to use technological advances and economic sanctions for the peril of humankind. Rather, they would be invited—as are we—into an initiation as emissaries of peace, where a spiritually intelligent expression of oneness, compassion, forgiveness and sharing of the world's wealth and resources govern decisions.

One of the world's greatest spiritual and social radicals was Jesus the Christ. He drew the attention of the ruling parties because he had the inner courage to go counter-culture through his inner realization of oneness with God. His integrative power and consciousness of unconditional love stood up to the political status quo of his time. He demonstrated how spirituality conquers the fiercest foes. Nelson Mandela spent twenty-seven years in prison while his people were awash in a civil bloodbath. Upon his release from prison, Mandela's actions of forgiveness and compassionate justice over retaliation moved his society towards healing, freedom and restoration. That choice is available to us all.

Patriotism, *Webster's Dictionary* tell us, is "devoted love, support and defense of one's country; national loyalty." It is the nationalistic aspect of patriotism that presents a slippery slope when used in conjunction with the attitude that one's nation and its needs should be considered above the rest of the world's. Genuine patriotism encompasses loyalty to the truth that the planet is comprised of one global family. We express true patriotism by our individual willingness to become spiritually integral beings, revealing an inner self-light and pouring it into every action from the pure realization of our oneness with all life. *This is what will bring a trans-*

formation of world-consciousness and therefore world-action.

We can see that the general tendency of the individual is to create his/her world from a reaction/response to what comes into their life from the outside. We see this reflected in the collective reactions of societies and governments: when someone verbally insults you, you insult back. When someone bombs your country, you bomb back. It's all from the outside. As we individually evolve in consciousness, we will begin to impact our individual world from the *inside* through the use of our spiritual knowledge and power thereby bringing the joy and peace from the within to the without. When enough individuals evolve through spiritual realization, a magnetic field will be created that attracts world leaders who reflect their awareness of the interconnectedness of life, and they will manifest it from the within to the without.

This evolved state of consciousness contains no need for strife between one's one good and the good of others because it is one-and-the-same Good! In the consciousness of oneness, there is no place for a limited self; there is all the space necessary for the expansive Self which is our natural state of oneness with all creation.

Moving from an Egocentric to a Worldcentric Point of View

As we set aside our human opinions and look through the lens of Divine Mind at those who are in the forefront of the great drama unfolding before us, let us practice affirming that Infinite Wisdom guides President Bush, his advisors, the government of Pakistan, our allies, and that the energetic of transformation guides Osama Bin Laden. Accepting the inherent soul-goodness residing within each individual—no matter how dim it seems to be—we accelerate the action of Truth within them. Then perhaps instead of winning wars we will begin winning hearts over to peace. When humanity's view transforms egocentric boundaries of "me and mine" into a worldcentric view of "ours" we have a true chance not only to create integrative policies of peace but to live them. Events such as the world is currently experiencing offer the prospect of moving into a creative response, one that we may have never before considered.

Duane Elgin, the renowned scientist and environmental activist, informs us that more than half of the world's population lives on less than $3.00 per day, goes without shelter, has no sanitation, does not get one clean glass of water and receives no education. It is his estimation that it would take approximately $40 million per year to build water systems in developing countries, to provide food, clothing, shelter and education. Can your inner vision see the possibility of emissaries of peace exercising their integrative power to create a quantum field of cosmic citizenship so strong that its contagion causes a radical change in how the world comprehends its interconnection and thus distributes its resources? *Can you see yourself as that very emissary of peace?* It is not redundant to say that it begins within individual consciousness, because *how we govern our individual lives determines the international character.*

Practicing Radical Love and Compassion

There is perhaps no teaching of Jesus' that presents more challenge to us than the command to "Love thine enemies and pray for those who persecute you." His admonition is not conditional; it is absolute. Forgiveness is a precursor to loving the enemy. Dr. Martin Luther King tells us that the act of forgiving "must always be initiated by the person who has been wronged, the victim of some great hurt, the recipient of some tortuous injustice, the absorber of some terrible act of oppression. Without this, no man can love his enemies. The degree to which we are able to forgive determines the degree to which we are able to love our enemies."

The Dalai Lama has said that the radicalism of the twenty-first century is compassion. Forgiving and loving our enemies means we have compassion for the perpetrators of insane violence—not condoning it in any way, but having compassion for persons who would participate in such bloodcurdling acts. We must hear the inner cries of the seeming enemy and be big enough to offer them a healing that is only found through love. What do I mean by "love"?

I mean the impersonal love for the soul that God created. It is what Gandhi and Jesus practiced in separating the doer from the deed—"Forgive them, for they know not what they do." Blessing the enemy is the practice of Universal Spiritual Principle.

The things that the Spirit is giving me to share are not necessarily the "feel good" aspects of the spiritual path, but it is time to grow up and grow deep in the only real security that there is: the God-Presence found in divine communion with the Infinite. When we deeply meditate and pray, we contact the Divine within us. Living in our consciousness of God-contact, we learn to see the face of the Infinite in all faces and love all beings as our own. We then love with the love of God, and it becomes possible to forgive "seventy times seven." *Intellectual acceptance or mere belief of this is not enough! We must—each of us—touch and directly commune with our depth of being, our Christ-consciousness.*

It is clear that returning hate for hate only multiplies hate. Darkness cannot be illuminated by more darkness. One must bring in the light. In our world community we have come to a place where it is inescapable not to love, forgive or reconcile with our so-called enemies. Hate is as equally injurious to the person who hates, to the nation that promotes hatred. Hate creates toxins within the international bloodstream. We can no longer ignore that hate divides and love unites. Love is the only force capable of transforming. *"Of all weapons,"* said Dr. Howard Thurman, *"love is the most deadly and devastating, and few there be who dare trust their fate in its hands."*

Love is not some impractical, utopian concept. An emissary of peace should be encouraged by the truth that the creative force of Love is the most enduring power in the world! May we in the twenty-first century heed the words and follow the example of those who have gone before us preaching and practicing love, compassion and forgiveness. Without making a declaration of peace within ourselves, our hearts cannot be prepared to embrace all humanity.

Teaching Our Children International Patriotism

I appreciated First Lady Laura Bush encouraging people not to allow children to watch every television report and be filled with images of war, but instead to take them aside and comfort them, to teach them about love. She said something powerful, and her advice is worth following. Sit with your families, hold them and tell them how much you love them. Pray together.

When there is peace in the family home, when spiritual principles are taught and practiced together, it becomes reflected in a child's attitude and behavior. When teaching children to pray, wise is the parent who instructs them to include the well-being of all the world's people in their prayers. Teach them to be proud that they have been made in the image and likeness of God, created out of love.

We must teach international patriotism in our schools. Nationality, race, color, gender—these are not adequate measurements of pride! Children should remain free from prejudice. Equality cannot be accepted by force; it must be born of true brotherly and sisterly love planted in the fertile soil of the receptive minds of children. **Children must be reminded that they are international citizens, that the entire world is their home and to compassionately accept responsibility for global care.**

Vision-birthing a Revolution of Values

There is a growing recognition that violence, war and prejudice offer no wisdom, no love, no justice, no peace or compassion to our world. Look back through time and you will see that hatred and war have left countries tattered with devastation! When there is violence flowing through the international bloodstream its toxins of ignorance upset the organic balance of the whole. **We are to connect the global heart to the global brain and put an end to the ignorance of hatred and violence that cause human suffering.**

Earlier this year Dr. John Hagelin, the world renowned quantum physicist who ran for President of the United States, spoke at the Agape International Spiritual Center. In his book, *Manual for a Perfect Government*, he expresses this wisdom: "...the experience of pure consciousness corresponds to the direct subjective experience of the unified field of all the laws of nature at the foundation of the physical universe. The influence of positivity and coherence generated by such group practice thus represents an actual physical influence of peace more powerful than any previous defensive technology. If, according to the UNESCO Charter, 'War begins in the minds of men,' then it can easily end in the far more fundamental experience of pure consciousness which underlies and unites us all. The most straightforward, practical implementation of this approach is to establish a 'prevention wing of the military' trained in peace-creating technologies..."

I love watching how the One Mind works! I was a guest on a radio program with Matthew Fox and Barbara Marx Hubbard. As we were invited to share, we realized each of us carried this same vision: As President Bush calls together his generals, a call would simultaneously go out to the peacemakers—what we call social architects—so that they may offer an approach that balances the military counsel to our nation's leaders. Not surprisingly, this was in alignment with Nelson Mandela's suggestion that our heads of state not only gather our best generals, but also our best mediators and negotiators. The Dalai Lama recommends the formation of an international council of sages wherein each country would elect representatives who were neither government officials or politicians, but individuals with genuine concern for regional, national and international affairs, those who consider war the last option, not the first.

When we examine the lives of those who have stood and continue to stand against ignorance, we see that they do not keep wisdom, philosophy or spirituality merely on the levels of intellect or belief. It is an understanding from within that gives them the strength to honor and live with impeccable integrity their commitment to humankind. True agents of change such as Mahatma Gandhi, Dr. Martin Luther King, Nelson Mandela and Mother Teresa demonstrate to the entire world that when the heart is disciplined it has no personal ambition except to be an instrument of peace and love.

The equality, dignity and freedom for which these great ones so passionately lived was for all humanity. Their lives were living proof of the truth that if we want to have more peace we must have more love. That is why to this day we speak of them as great lovers of humankind. In their meditations and prayers they were flooded with the Light of Divine Love and joined the ranks of emissaries of peace who changed the time in which they lived and yet live. You are a choice-point in the center of the universe. What will be your choice? Are you willing to be a blessing to the planet?

To have more love we must understand as they did that our true nature is love. To discern that our true nature is love is to know that we are created in the very image and likeness of Love, which is the Essence of Life itself.

Speaking the Language of Love

Love is always the winning argument; violence is the language of the inarticulate! The world is teetering on the precipice of its next level of evolution. "War will cease," Dr. Ernest Holmes tells us, "not when God decides this for us, but when enough people know that it is no longer desirable, and steadfastly maintain their position. From communion with Spirit man will come to perceive the deeper Reality, the broader sharing of the human experience." Jesus exhorted, "Put your sword back into its place; for all who take the sword will perish by the sword." Old structures are falling apart and the Spirit is calling us to express the natural love, peace and compassion of the soul.

Speaking for myself, what I know to do is to keep meditating, keep praying, keep opening my heart wider and wider, keep listening more deeply. I am going to love more profoundly and express more compassionately. This is my contribution as I walk the path of an emissary of peace, a cosmic citizen. I am committed to being, saying and doing what is necessary to create the kind of world I want to live in.

I invite you look into your own heart and sense its wisdom instructing you in the ways of peace, forgiveness, compassion and unconditional love.

I would like to share with you a letter that was written to the one hundred and twenty-four of us who recently returned from a spiritual pilgrimage to Egypt, just before the tragic events of September 11th. It was written by Amir, one of our Muslim tour guides. It is a heart-moving reminder that there is truly no distance between souls.

To all my friends in the U.S.,

I have been watching the news for three hours, not believing what has happened. This is a real bad time for innocence and security and I am feeling for everyone in the world. I cannot understand how anyone called human could do that.

I want you to know that I am thinking of you, and I will remember every one of you in my prayers as a Muslim. I am so afraid for everyone in the Middle East, especially here in the Motherland. I will be praying for tolerance, wisdom, peace and understanding for your leaders. I am going to find my faith that in all destruction there is always new life. Peace and blessings to my friends.

Please, I consider all of Agape people responsible for spreading the word around that we in the Middle East do not do such a thing in Islam. It does not encourage such lunatic acts of murder.

All my love and support for everyone of you.
Amir

Tools of an Emissary of Peace

What follows are what I call tools of an emissary of peace, practices I have found supportive in my own personal *sadhana*. Prayer, meditation, affirmations—these train us to tangibly commune with the Eternal Presence within our souls, to skillfully co-create our human incarnation. Depending on what my inward experience is, I choose from among these techniques, or, on occasion, use all three! (And, although it is not described in this writing, chanting is also a powerful healer I often call upon.)

I want to remind you that these tools are to be used with loving patience. Awakening, insight, awareness—these cannot be forced. Yet the more we practice, with every step we take on the path of an emissary of peace, we draw closer to self-realization, to seeing with inward sight what has been true about us since the beginning of time. Even if we haven't yet reached the highest pinnacle of spiritual awakening, it is perfectly appropriate to claim our inherent state of enlightenment through prayer and affirmations. These practices give us the courage, endurance, joy and steadfastness necessary for an emissary of peace not to give up on himself/herself, or anyone else.

For our purpose here, the following affirmations, prayer and meditation and are directed towards the painful challenges we have been walking through together since September 11th. You may, however, adapt them for any purpose.

Affirmations of an Emissary of Peace

When to practice: The time to practice an affirmation is whenever you need to! This practice is not limited to challenging times—it is effective under all circumstances of life. Affirmations are especially powerful immediately upon waking up in the morning and just before falling asleep at night when the subjective mind is open and receptive. In the deep stillness of meditation, when the superconscious mind is accessed, is also a beneficial time for affirming spiritual truth.

How to practice: Affirmations can be made formally and informally—sitting on a meditation cushion or riding in the bus. Formal affirmations are made intentionally, meaning one sits with the intention to practice affirmations. Informal affirmations may be made in daily circumstances to which you wish to apply an immediate spiritual response—a rising to the need of the moment with a spiritualized consciousness. Since the practice of informal affirmation is obvious, we will address in more detail the technique of formal affirmation.

You may prepare your affirmations ahead of time,

or, invite them to arise in your consciousness as you sit in the stillness. If you don't already have a space in your home set aside for prayer and meditation, choose a spot conducive to quiet.

Sitting on a chair or on the floor, take a position of potency, keeping your back straight and chin parallel to the floor. Now, take a deep inhalation and make a full exhalation. Relax into the breath, keeping the mind alert so you don't fall asleep. At first, repeat your affirmation aloud a few times so that you may hear and feel the conviction of your faith. Then say it more slowly and softly, until it gradually becomes only a mental affirmation. Mentally repeat it until there is a sense of peace, which is the first sign that your subjective mind is vibrating in sync with your Word, which is Spirit in you.

As I mentioned, the following examples are affirmative statements that may assist you in processing the tragic events of September 11th; please tailor them to your personal needs.

I free myself from the need to judge any person, nation or event. My consciousness is at peace, for it is now rooted and grounded in the Spirit. My thinking is premised on Infinite Mind and I am estab-

lished in love, compassion and forgiveness.

From the center of my heart, I radiate compassion to all beings knowing that their pain is bathed in the Infinite Love of the Spirit.

I awaken the spirit of forgiveness within me. Even now it fills my consciousness with loving kindness towards myself and all beings. I judge not, lest I be judged. I love with the unconditional love of God.

Right here, right now, Divine Love loves through me. Divine Right Action frees me from the errors of human judgment and causes me to know that all beings are emanations of the One Life.

The true spiritual essence is all I know of each person. I think rightly, and I love greatly. I love to let Love express through me.

I accept the fullness of life and am a distribution center of compassion, forgiveness, and love. I am blessed and prospered by Divine Love as it flows through me now.

I declare my faith in God and release material patterns of behavior. I know that God is at the center of Life and I depend upon That which projected all creation as its own to be the Source of eternal safety and security for all beings.

Prayer of an Emissary of Peace

We pray because it is a natural flow of communication with the Soul of our Souls—a love-flood of praise, gratitude, surrender, abandon, joy, agony—the full spectrum of feelings filled with the confidence that God listens to the heart. Prayer, also, is formal and informal. There is the more formal scientific form of prayer such as Spiritual Mind Treatment as practiced in the Science of Mind and Spirit, and there is the informal prayer spoken in the language of the heart. The point here is sincerity. Many people declare their belief in God, but first rely on material help in challenging situations and pray as a last resort. An emissary of peace enters a prayerful state first!

The following combines both formal and informal prayer in sweet communion with the personal and impersonal aspects of the Spirit.

Right here and right now I recognize the God-Power, the God-Presence that is my very life, my very being. I feel so unified with this Presence. Something cries out from the depth of my being: I am what Thou art, Thou art what I am. There is no separation, no otherness. It is from this centeredness that I recognize that God is Love. And so I embrace myself right where I am. In full acknowledgment of the tragedy that has impacted our world, I wrap my arms around these events, around the international heartbreak taking place on the planet.

I speak the word now, knowing that it is a law unto itself that knows its own fulfillment. In perfect confidence I call forth the perfect peace that passeth human understanding. I know the people of all nations, the leaders of all nations to be wrapped in that peace right now. I embrace all individuals who are in pain now, including myself. I announce to all, "Peace, be still." I know that right in the midst of grief, anger, fear, guilt—right in the midst of this the all-loving, all-knowing Spirit is uplifting, healing and transforming the lives of all people—those who are grieving, those who perpetrated the grief, and the leaders of all nations. This prayer is healing the global family. Right now I am being lifted into the understanding that the Most High is our habitation so no permanent hurt, harm or danger can come near our dwelling place.

Oh Father-Mother-God, how great Thou art. The anguish of those who suffer has broken open my *heart and the hearts of all in compassionate awareness and willingness to be a place of peace on the planet. In an embrace of loving compassion I hold all those who have shuffled off the physical form in the World Trade Center, the Pentagon and Pennsylvania. I declare their aliveness in You. Fire cannot burn the soul, water cannot drown it—for eternal beings are we all. I give thanks for the realization that life is eternal. I embrace the loved ones who are left behind knowing that the healing balm of peace is finding its way into their hearts.*

In this pure awareness, I let it be. And so it is.

Meditation of an Emissary of Peace

In the words of Dr. Ernest Holmes, "Meditation is for the purpose of inbreathing the Essence of Reality," which is our divinity. Buddhists, Christians, Hindus, religions of indigenous peoples—all have their techniques of meditation. An emissary of peace adopts such a practice to experience the union that is never broken between the individual soul and the Over Soul. This oneness is the Essence of the Reality of our existence. As with affirmation and prayer, meditation also has more than one form. The following is a guided meditation on forgiveness.

To begin its practice, sit in a position of potency with your back straight, yet relaxed. If you are sitting on a chair, place your feet flat on the floor. With your hands facing upwards in a mode of receptivity—or downward to inhibit distraction, gently close your eyes and begin to breathe in your natural rhythm. As you become aware of your breath, know Infinite Life is breathing you. As you feel your heartbeat, know the Divine Heart is beating as your own. If you go deep enough to hear the circulation of your blood, know that it is Spirit circulating throughout your bloodstream.

Begin to relate intimately to That which is nearer than the nearest, dearer than the dearest, closer than your neck vein. This Omnipresent Lover is aware of you. It has a personal love for you so great that it personalized itself as you! Sense this now and let it open the floodgates of your heart. Unarmor your consciousness by acknowledging that the Spirit loves all created beings with this same intensity—the seeming saint and sinner alike. Accept for yourself and for all beings the compassion, mercy and unconditional love of God. Do not be surprised if tears arise—there is no inappropriate emotion because the Spirit can handle everything!

Whisper within to yourself: *I am willing to heal those places within myself that are fearful, ashamed, angry. Right now I make room in my heart for my pain, and for the pain of all beings. We float in a sea of oneness. We are not we but One. In that oneness, I embrace you who have left this three-dimensional planet so unexpectedly. I send to your souls Godspeed, love, goodwill as you acclimate to a new dimension of life. I send peace to your loved ones on this side of the veil and a vibration of healing to their hearts.*

Strike a mystic chord in memory of a time when loving kindness was expressed perfectly through you. With the next out-breath whisper within: *May all beings be at peace. May peace infiltrate the hearts of those who perpetrated hatred and violence. They are in need of healing and I offer it now in forgiveness and compassion. May they heal into their true nature. May they experience the transforming knowledge that sets them free, free from the desire to harm. As they are forgiven by the Spirit, so do I in my own heart forgive them.*

I forgive myself for any way in which I knowingly or unknowingly caused hurt or harm to any living being or creature. I forgive all who have ever hurt or harmed me. Everything between us is now cleared up. I am free and they are free, free in the Freedom of the Spirit.

Let the breath continue to flow in its natural rhythm. Continue extending to yourself and all beings vibrations of forgiveness, mercy, peace and loving kindness.

When you bring your meditation to a close, don't arise from your meditation cushion until you ask the Spirit to reveal to you your part in Divine Right

Action. Carry the aftereffects of your meditation into your activities, offering to all whom you meet peace, joy, and love. Support your meditative efforts with prayer and affirmations, practicing the presence of God throughout your day. Then you will be a beneficial presence on the planet, going forth into your day with the song of God in your heart.

About the Author

Dr. Michael Beckwith is the Founder and Spiritual Director of one of the world's largest and rapidly expanding spiritual communities, the Agape International Spiritual Center, located in Culver City, California. A pioneering organization in the New Thought-Ancient Wisdom tradition of spirituality and philosophy, the Agape community has 8,000 members and thousands of friends worldwide.

Agape is the result Dr. Beckwith's own explorations in the emergence of consciousness. As a freshman student at Morehouse College, he was exposed to the Christian mysticism of the beloved philosopher and humanitarian Dr. Howard Thurman. Insightful glimpses into the spiritual realm, familiar to him since childhood, were given credence and encouragement to flourish. By the time he transferred to the University of Southern California, he began to experience conscious jolts of spiritual awakening. Led to discard a traditional college curriculum, he entered a period of intense study of Eastern religion, Western mysticism and the practice of meditation, culminating in his enrollment in the Ernest Holmes Institute of Consciousness Studies.

Dr. Beckwith's soul-life married East and West, which today is one of the distinguishing hallmarks of his unique transdenominational Agape International Spiritual Center. His all-embracing approach is born of a coherent vision which honors and incorporates time-tested methods of affirmative prayer and meditation passed down from the traditions of Bhagavan Krishna, Gautama Buddha, Jesus the Christ and spiritual masters of contemporary times.

In 1986, Dr. Beckwith's inner vision revealed a world united on an ethical basis of humankind's highest development spiritually, philosophically, educationally, culturally, scientifically and socially. Applying a visioning technique originated by Dr. Beckwith, committed associates came forward to participate in his vision, resulting in the formation of the Agape International Spiritual Center. Now, just fifteen years later, Agape facilitates a network of twenty ministries, some of which feed the homeless, serve prisoners and their families, provide hospice and grief support, partner with community organizations and programs which advocate the preservation of the planet's environmental resources.

Dr. Beckwith serves as National Co-chair of "A Season for Nonviolence," an international movement founded in partnership with Arun Gandhi, founder of the M. K. Gandhi Institute for Nonviolence. "Season" promotes and teaches the principles of *ahimsa*, nonviolence, practiced by Mahatma Gandhi and Dr. Martin Luther King. He is a founding member of the Association for Global New Thought, which yearly convenes "The Synthesis Dialogues" with His Holiness the Dalai Lama.

Thousands gather at the Agape International Spiritual Center on Wednesdays and Sundays to learn from Dr. Beckwith's spiritual connection to the timeless realm, as he shares in a down-to-earth style timely truths applicable to twenty-first century living. His is a passionately unique voice, announcing to all that they are a beloved and essential part of the Universe.

For information about Dr. Beckwith's availability as a speaker, keynote conference speaker, retreat facilitator, or to conduct a seminar on his unique visioning technique, please call (310) 348-1250. Or write to: Dr. Michael Beckwith, Agape International Spiritual Center, 5700 Buckingham Parkway, Culver City, CA 90230, USA.

Dr. Beckwith's book, *Forty Day Mind Fast Soul Feast*, may be ordered from the Agape Quiet Mind Bookstore at the address given above or from their website: www.agapeonline.org